Preparing for Disasters for People with Disabilities and other Special Needs

Together, we can save a life

Visit the websites listed below to obtain additional information:

www.access-board.gov	The Access Board
www.aoa.dhhs.gov	DHHS Administration on Aging
www.ncd.gov	National Council on Disability
www.nod.org/emergency	National Organization on Disability
www.prepare.org	Prepare.org
www.aapd.com	American Association for People with Disabilities
www.afb.org	American Foundation for the Blind
www.nad.org	National Association of the Deaf
www.lacity.org/DOD	Los Angeles City Department on Disability
www.easter-seals.org	Easter Seals

For more in-depth information, get a copy of "Disaster Preparedness for People with Disabilities" (A5091) from the American Red Cross, or visit www.redcross.org/services/disaster/beprepared/disability.pdf

For the millions of Americans who have physical, medical, sensory or cognitive disabilities, emergencies such as fires, floods and acts of terrorism present a real challenge. The same challenge also applies to the elderly and other special needs populations. Protecting yourself and your family when disaster strikes requires planning ahead. This booklet will help you get started. Discuss these ideas with your family, friends and/or your personal care attendant, or anyone else in your support network and prepare an emergency plan. Post the plan where everyone will see it, keep a copy with you and make sure everyone involved in your plan has a copy.

WHY PREPARE?

Where will you, your family, your friends or personal care attendants be when an emergency or disaster strikes?

You, and those you care about, could be anywhere – at home, work, school or in transit. How will you find each other? Will you know your loved ones will be safe?

Emergencies and disasters can strike quickly and without warning and can force you to evacuate your neighborhood or confine you to your home. What would you do if basic services – water, gas, electricity or telephones – were cut off?

Local officials and relief workers will be on the scene after a disaster, but they cannot reach everyone right away.

You are in the best position to plan for your own safety as you are best able to know your functional abilities and possible needs during and after an emergency or disaster situation. You can cope with disaster by preparing in advance with your family and care attendants. You will need to create a personal support network and complete a personal assessment. You will also need to follow the four preparedness steps listed in this booklet.

1. Get informed
2. Make a plan
3. Assemble a kit
4. Maintain your plan and kit

Knowing what to do is your best protection and your responsibility.

What You Need to Do

CREATE A PERSONAL SUPPORT NETWORK

A personal support network (sometimes called a self-help team) can help you prepare for a disaster. They can do this by helping you identify and get the resources you need to cope effectively. Network members can also assist you after a disaster happens.

Organize a network that includes your home, school, workplace, volunteer site, and any other places where you spend a lot of time. Members of your network can be roommates, relatives, neighbors, friends, and co-workers. They should be people you trust and who can check to see if you need assistance. They should know your capabilities and needs, and be able to provide help within minutes.

Do not depend on only one person. Include a minimum of three people in your network for each location where you regularly spend a lot of time since people work different shifts, take vacations and are not always available.

COMPLETE A PERSONAL ASSESSMENT

Decide what you will be able to do for yourself and what assistance you may need before, during and after a disaster. This will be based on the environment after the disaster, your capabilities and your limitations.

To complete a personal assessment, make a list of your personal needs and your resources for meeting them in a disaster environment. Think about the following questions and note your answers in writing or record them on a tape cassette that you will share with your network. These answers should describe both your current capabilities and the assistance you will need. Base your plan on your lowest anticipated level of functioning.

Daily Living

- **Personal Care**
 Do you regularly need assistance with personal care, such as bathing and grooming? Do you use adaptive equipment to help you get dressed?

- **Water Service**
 What will you do if water service is cut off for several days or if you are unable to heat water?

- **Personal Care Equipment**
 Do you use a shower chair, tub-transfer bench or other similar equipment?

- **Adaptive Feeding Devices**
 Do you use special utensils that help you prepare or eat food independently?

- **Electricity-Dependent Equipment**
 How will you continue to use equipment that runs on electricity, such as dialysis, electrical lifts, etc.? Do you have a safe back-up power supply and how long will it last?

Getting Around

- **Disaster Debris**
 How will you cope with the debris in your home or along your planned exit route following the disaster?

- **Transportation**
 Do you need a specially equipped vehicle or accessible transportation?

- **Errands**
 Do you need help to get groceries, medications and medical supplies? What if your caregiver cannot reach you because roads are blocked or the disaster has affected him or her as well?

Evacuating

- **Building Evacuation**
  Do you need help to leave your home or office? Can you reach and activate an alarm? Will you be able to evacuate independently without relying on auditory cues (such as noise from a machine near the stairs – these cues may be absent if the electricity is off or alarms are sounding)?

- **Building Exits**
  Are there other exits (stairs, windows or ramps) if the elevator is not working or cannot be used? Can you read emergency signs in print or Braille? Do emergency alarms have audible and visible features (marking escape routes and exits) that will work even if electrical service is disrupted?

- **Getting Help**
  How will you call or summon for the help you will need to leave the building? Do you know the locations of text telephones and phones that have amplification? Will your hearing aids work if they get wet from emergency sprinklers? Have you determined how to communicate with emergency personnel if you don't have an interpreter, your hearing aids aren't working, or if you don't have a word board or other augmentative communication device?

- **Mobility Aids / Ramp Access**
  What will you do if you cannot find your mobility aids? What will you do if your ramps are shaken loose or become separated from the building?

- **Service Animals/Pets**
  Will you be able to care for your animal (provide food, shelter, veterinary attention, etc.) during and after a disaster? Do you have another caregiver for your animal if you are unable to meet its needs? Do you have the appropriate licenses for your service animal so you will be permitted to keep it with you should you need or choose to use an emergency public shelter?

1. GET INFORMED

Contact your local emergency management office or American Red Cross Chapter to gather information you will need to create a plan.

♦ **Community Hazards.** Ask about the specific hazards that threaten your community (e.g. hurricanes, tornados, earthquakes) and about your risk from those hazards. Additionally, hazard information for your local area can be obtained at www.hazardmaps.gov.

♦ **Community Disaster Plans.** Learn about community response plans, evacuation plans and designated emergency shelters. Ask about the emergency plans and procedures that exist in places you and your family spend time such as places of employment, schools and child care centers. If you do not own a vehicle or drive, find out in advance what your community's plans are for evacuating those without private transportation.

♦ **Community Warning Systems.** Find out how local authorities will warn you of a pending disaster and how they will provide information to you during and after a disaster. Learn about NOAA Weather Radio and its alerting capabilities (www.noaa.gov).

♦ **Assistance Programs.** Ask about special assistance programs available in the event of an emergency. Many communities ask people with a disability to register, usually with the local fire or police department, or the local emergency management office so needed help can be provided quickly in an emergency. Let your personal care attendant know you have registered, and with whom. If you are electric-dependent, be sure to register with your local utility company.

2. Make a Plan

Because a disaster can disrupt your primary emergency plan, it is also important for you to develop a back-up plan to ensure your safety.

- **Meet with Your Family/Personal Care Attendants/Building Manager.** Review the information you gathered about community hazards and emergency plans.

- **Choose an "Out-of-Town" Contact.** Ask an out-of-town friend or relative to be your contact. Following a disaster, family members should call this person and tell them where they are. Everyone must know the contact's phone numbers. After a disaster, it is often easier to make a long distance call than a local call from a disaster area.

- **Decide Where to Meet.** In the event of an emergency, you may become separated from household members. Choose a place right outside your home in case of a sudden emergency, like a fire. Choose a location outside your neighborhood in case you can't return home.

- **Complete a Communications Plan.** Your plan should include contact information for family members, members of your support network, caregivers, work, and school. Your plan should also include information for your out-of-town contact, meeting locations, emergency services, and the National Poison Control Center (1-800-222-1222). A form for recording this information can be found at www.ready.gov - or at www.redcross.org/contactcard. These websites also provide blank wallet cards on which contact information can be recorded and carried in a wallet, purse, backpack, etc, for quick reference. Teach your children how to call the emergency phone numbers and when it is appropriate to do so. Be sure each family member has a copy of your communication plan and post it near your telephone for use in an emergency.

- **Escape Routes and Safe Places.** In a fire or other emergency, you may need to evacuate on a moment's notice. Be ready to get out fast. Be sure everyone in your family knows the best escape routes out of your home as well as where the safe places are in your home for each type of disaster (i.e., if a tornado approaches, go to the basement or the lowest floor of your home or an interior room or closet with no windows).

Use a blank sheet of paper to draw the floor plans of your home. Show the location of doors, windows, stairways, large furniture, your disaster supplies kit, fire extinguisher, smoke alarms, other visual and auditory alarms, collapsible ladders, first-aid kits, and utility shut-off points. Show important points outside such as garages, patios, stairways, elevators, driveways, and porches.

Indicate at least two escape routes from each room, and mark a place outside of the home where household members and/or your personal care attendant should meet in case of fire. If you or

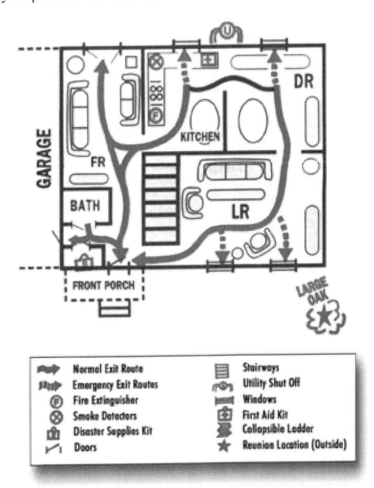

someone in your household uses a wheelchair, make exits from your home wheelchair accessible.

Practice emergency evacuation drills at least two times a year, but as often as you update your escape plan. Be sure to include family and/or your personal care attendant in the drills.

- **Plan for Your Pets**. Take your pets with you if you evacuate. However, be aware that pets (other than service animals) usually are not permitted in emergency public shelters for health reasons. Prepare a list of family, friends, boarding facilities, veterinarians, and "pet-friendly" hotels that could shelter your pets in an emergency.

- **Prepare for Different Hazards**. Include in your plan how to prepare for each hazard that could impact your local community and how to protect yourself. For instance, most people shelter in a basement when there is a tornado warning, but most basements are not wheelchair-accessible. Determine in advance what your alternative shelter will be and how you will get there. Other hazards, like a home fire, will require you to leave. Make sure both primary and secondary exits are accessible and that you can locate them by touch or feel (since lights may be out and thick, black smoke may make it very hard to see). Reference the websites listed on the back cover to learn more about the different actions required for different hazards.

Action Checklist – Items To Do Before a Disaster

☐ **Considerations for people with disabilities**

Those with disabilities or other special needs often have unique needs that require more detailed planning in the event of a disaster. Consider the following actions as you prepare:

- Learn what to do in case of power outages and personal injuries. Know how to connect and start a back-up power supply for essential medical equipment.
- Consider getting a medical alert system that will allow you to call for help if you are immobilized in an emergency. Most alert systems require a working phone line, so have a back-up plan, such as a cell phone or pager, if the regular landlines are disrupted.
- If you use an electric wheelchair or scooter, have a manual wheelchair for backup.
- Teach those who may need to assist you in an emergency how to operate necessary equipment. Also, label equipment and attach laminated instructions for equipment use.
- Store back-up equipment (mobility, medical, etc.) at your neighbor's home, school, or your workplace.
- Arrange for more than one person from your personal support network to check on you in an emergency, so there is at least one back-up if the primary person you rely on cannot.
- If you are vision impaired, deaf or hard of hearing, plan ahead for someone to convey essential emergency information to you if you are unable to use the TV or radio.
- If you use a personal care attendant obtained from an agency, check to see if the agency has special provisions for emergencies (e.g., providing services at another location should an evacuation be ordered).
- If you live in an apartment, ask the management to identify and mark accessible exits and access to all areas designated for emergency shelter or safe rooms. Ask about plans for alerting and evacuating those with sensory disabilities.
- Have a cell phone with an extra battery. If you are unable to get out of a building, you can let someone know where you are and guide them to you. Keep the numbers you may need to call with you if the 9-1-1 emergency number is overloaded.

- Learn about devices and other technology available (PDA's, text radio, pagers, etc.) to assist you in receiving emergency instructions and warnings from local officials.
- Be prepared to provide clear, specific and concise instructions to rescue personnel. Practice giving these instructions (verbally, pre-printed phrases, word board, etc.) clearly and quickly.
- Prepare your personal support network to assist you with anticipated reactions and emotions associated with disaster and traumatic events (i.e. confusion, thought processing and memory difficulties, agitation, fear, panic, and anxiety).
- You don't have to be the only one prepared – encourage others to be prepared and consider volunteering or working with local authorities on disability and other special needs preparedness efforts.

☐ **Utilities**

Know how and when to turn off water, gas and electricity at the main switches or valves and share this information with your family and caregivers. Keep any tools you will need near gas and water shut off valves. Turn off the utilities only if you suspect the lines are damaged, you suspect a leak, or if local officials instruct you to do so.

(Note: Gas shut-off procedure - As part of the learning process, do not actually turn off the gas. If the gas is turned off for any reason, only a qualified professional can turn it back on. It might take several weeks for a professional to respond. In the meantime, you will require alternate sources to heat your home, make hot water and cook.)

☐ **Fire Extinguisher**
   Be sure everyone knows how to use your fire extinguishers (ABC type) and where they are kept.

☐ **Smoke Alarms**
   Install smoke alarms on each level of your home, especially near the bedrooms. Individuals with sensory disabilities should consider installing smoke alarms that have strobe lights and vibrating pads. Follow local codes and manufacturer's instructions about installation requirements. Also, consider installing a carbon monoxide alarm in your home.

☐ **Insurance Coverage**
   Check if you have adequate insurance coverage. Homeowners insurance does not cover flood damage and may not provide full coverage for other hazards. Talk with your insurance agent and make sure you have adequate coverage to protect your family against financial loss.

☐ **First Aid/CPR & AED (Automated External Defibrillation)**
   Take American Red Cross first aid and CPR/AED classes. Red Cross courses can accommodate people with disabilities. Discuss your needs when registering for the classes.

☐ **Inventory Home Possessions**
   Make a record of your possessions to help you claim reimbursement in case of loss or damage. Store this information in a safe

deposit box or other secure (flood/fire safe) location to ensure the records survive a disaster. Include photographs or video of the interior and exterior of your home as well as cars, boats and recreational vehicles. Also, have photos of durable medical equipment and be sure to make a record of the make and model numbers for each item. Get professional appraisals of jewelry, collectibles, artwork or other items that may be difficult to evaluate. Make copies of receipts and canceled checks showing the cost for valuable items.

☐ **Vital Records and Documents**
Vital family records and other important documents such as birth and marriage certificates, social security cards, passports, wills, deeds, and financial, insurance, and immunizations records should be kept in a safe deposit box or other safe location.

☐ **Reduce Home Hazards**
In a disaster, ordinary items in the home can cause injury and damage. Take these steps to reduce your risk.

- Keep the shut-off switch for oxygen equipment near your bed or chair, so you can get to it quickly if there is a fire.
- Have a professional repair defective electrical wiring and leaky gas connections.
- Place large, heavy objects on lower shelves, and hang pictures and mirrors away from beds.
- Use straps or other restraints to secure tall cabinets, bookshelves, large appliances (especially water heater, furnace and refrigerator), mirrors, shelves, large picture frames, and light fixtures to wall studs.
- Repair cracks in ceilings and foundations.
- Store weed killers, pesticides and flammable products away from heat sources.
- Place oily rags or waste in covered metal cans and dispose of them according to local regulations.
- Have a professional clean and repair chimneys, flue pipes, connectors, and gas vents.

3. ASSEMBLE A DISASTER SUPPLIES KIT

In the event you need to evacuate at a moment's notice and take essentials with you, you probably will not have the opportunity to shop or search for the supplies you and your family will need. Every household should assemble a disaster supplies kit and keep it up to date.

A disaster supplies kit is a collection of basic items a family would probably need to stay safe and be more comfortable during and after a disaster. Disaster supplies kit items should be stored in a portable container(s) as close as possible to the exit door. Review the contents of your kit at least once per year or as your family's needs change. Also, consider having emergency supplies in each vehicle and at your place of employment.

The following should be included in your basic disaster supplies kit:

- Three-day supply of nonperishable food and manual can opener.
- Three-day supply of water (one gallon of water per person, per day).
- Portable, battery-powered radio or television and extra batteries.
- Flashlight and extra batteries.
- First aid kit and manual.
- Sanitation and hygiene items (hand sanitizer, moist towelettes, and toilet paper).
- Matches in waterproof container.
- Whistle.
- Extra clothing and blankets.
- Kitchen accessories and cooking utensils.
- Photocopies of identification and credit cards.
- Cash and coins.
- Special needs items such as prescription medications, eye glasses, contact lens solution, and hearing aid batteries.
- Items for infants, such as formula, diapers, bottles, and pacifiers.
- Tools, pet supplies, a map of the local area, and other items to meet your unique family needs.

If you live in a cold climate, you must think about warmth. It is possible that you will not have heat during or after a disaster. Think about your clothing and bedding needs. Be sure to include one set of the following for each person:

- Jacket or coat.
- Long pants and long sleeve shirt.
- Sturdy shoes.
- Hat, mittens, and scarf.
- Sleeping bag or warm blanket.

Supplies for your vehicle include:

- Flashlight, extra batteries and maps.
- First aid kit and manual.
- White distress flag.
- Tire repair kit, booster/jumper cables, pump and flares.
- Bottled water and non-perishable foods such as granola bars.
- Seasonal supplies: Winter - blanket, hat, mittens, shovel, sand, tire chains, windshield scraper, florescent distress flag; Summer – sunscreen lotion (SPF 15 or greater), shade item (umbrella, wide brimmed hat, etc).

4. Maintain Your Plan

Quiz: Review your plan every six months and quiz your family about what to do.

Drill: Conduct fire and emergency evacuation drills on a regular basis with your family.

Restock: Check food supplies for expiration dates and discard, or replace stored water and food every six months.

Test: Read the indicator on your fire extinguisher(s) and follow the manufacturer's instructions to recharge. Test your smoke alarms monthly and change the batteries at least once a year. Replace alarms every 10 years.

Plan Maintenance Chart

Check off task and enter date performed:

	6 months	1 year	18 months	2 years
Review plan and quiz *Date*	☐	☐	☐	☐
Hold fire and emergency evacuation drills *Date*	☐	☐	☐	☐
Replace stored food and water *Date*	☐	☐	☐	☐
Check fire extinguishers and recharge *Date*	☐	☐	☐	☐

Smoke Alarm Maintenance Chart

Check off task and enter date performed:

Test monthly *Date*	☐	☐	☐	☐
Change batteries *Date*	☐	☐	☐	☐
Replace alarms *Date*	☐	☐	☐	☐

If Disaster Strikes

If you are instructed to take shelter immediately, do so at once

If you are instructed to evacuate

Should you need to leave, your first option and plan should always be to family or friends first; they can accommodate you, your pets, and help you be most comfortable  in a stressful situation. Emergency public shelters will be available, and can provide a safe place to stay and meals while you are there. However, they do not provide personal health care. If you require the care of a personal attendant and choose to go to a shelter, bring the attendant with you.

- Listen to the radio or television for the location of emergency shelters. Note those that are accessible to those with physical disabilities and those that have other disability friendly assistance features such as TTY lines.
- Shut off water, gas and electricity if instructed to do so and if time permits.
- Wear appropriate clothing and sturdy shoes.
- Take your disaster supplies kit.
- Lock your home.
- Use travel routes specified by local authorities and don't use shortcuts because certain areas may be impassable or dangerous.
- Confirm upon arrival at an emergency shelter that it can meet your special care needs.
- Inform members of your support network and out-of-town contact of your location and status.

Learn More

The Federal Emergency Management Agency's Community and Family Preparedness Program and American Red Cross Community Disaster Education are nationwide efforts to help people prepare for disasters of all types.

For more information, please contact your local emergency management office or American Red Cross chapter.

These publications are also available by calling FEMA at 1-800-480-2520, or writing:

> **FEMA**
> **P.O. Box 2012**
> **Jessup, MD 20794-2012**

Publications with an "A" number are available from your local American Red Cross chapter.

- Are You Ready? An In-depth Guide to Citizen Preparedness (IS-22)
- Preparing for Disaster (FEMA 475) (A4600)
- Food and Water in an Emergency (FEMA 477) (A5055)
- Helping Children Cope with Disaster (FEMA 478) (A4499)

FEMA 476
A4497
August 2004

Made in United States
Orlando, FL
30 April 2022